LifeCaps Presents:

Pope to the Poor

The Life and Times of Pope Francis (Jorge Mario Bergoglio)

By Paul Brody

BookCaps™ Study Guides
www.bookcaps.com

Cover Image © Iakov Kalinin - Fotolia.com

Table of Contents

About LifeCaps

LifeCaps is an imprint of BookCaps™ Study Guides. With each book, a lesser known or sometimes forgotten life is recapped. We publish a wide array of topics (from baseball and music to literature and philosophy), so check our growing catalogue regularly (**www.bookcaps.com**) to see our newest books.

Introduction

On March 13, 2013, at 7:06 pm (Central European Time), white smoke was spotted rising from the chimney of the Sistine Chapel where the conclave was being held. It could only mean one thing -- a new pope had been chosen to lead the Catholic Church. Although many did not know the name of Jorge Mario Bergoglio, the Cardinal from Argentina, as he was not predicted to be the new pope by any of the analysts or even administrators of the church, the world quickly began to praise him for his extremely humble attitude and straightforward manner. News headlines exploded with information about the first non-European and first Jesuit pope in the history of the church, and Latin Americans rejoiced at finally having significant representation in the church hierarchy.

Succeeding the previous Pope Benedict XVI at seventy six years old, Bergoglio steps up to the plate at a tumultuous time in history of the Catholic Church. He is the new leader of a church that has been plagued by a decreasing number of priests as well as members, numerous sex scandals, and calls for reform. His election comes as such a surprise because many believed that the conclave would choose a young, vibrant cardinal to help bring new life into the church. While he is no longer young, Bergoglio is not against changing the traditions of Catholic Church and is already notable for bringing many new "firsts" into the papacy.

A man of humble beginnings, Jorge Mario Bergoglio is the descendant of an Italian immigrant family. Extremely intelligent, academic and spiritual, with strong traditional values, he decided to join the church at a young age. His early life and experiences have shaped Bergoglio's views about poverty and gave him a great respect for the working class and the unemployed. These views have defined his entire life's work and will follow him as his new status as pope is cemented and he begins to have more and more influence in the Catholic Church.

Even though he is now one of the most powerful religious figures in the world, the new Pope Francis still acts as if he is just like everybody else and perhaps that is part of his charm. He speaks simply and in a conversational manner, purposefully avoids the luxurious housing, dress and manner of the Vatican and uses social media such as Twitter. Somewhat shy and with a dry sense of humor, Bergoglio enjoys reading the newspaper and listening to classical music on the radio. As a young man, he loved to tango, and the newspapers were quick to point out his lifelong passion for soccer, and ongoing support of the San Lorenzo soccer club.

This biography will follow Bergoglio's ancestors as they travel by ship from Italy to Buenos Aires, explore Jorge's career as priest, bishop, and later cardinal, delve deep into his beliefs and opinions about the world and the state of the church, as well as attempt to predict how this man from humble beginnings will help shape the Catholic Church in the future.

Chapter 1: Early Life and Education

Family and Childhood

The Bergoglio family, including Jorge's grandmother and father, arrived at the port of Buenos Aires in January of 1929. They had decided to take the risk and immigrate to the Americas from Italy in order to make something of themselves. At the time, Italy was still recovering from the World War and its economy was in an unhealthy state. There was not much opportunity for advancement or many good jobs available. The Americas offered a brand new start, and the promise of better, more plentiful jobs, a good education, and social mobility. Several other members of the Bergoglio family had already immigrated to Buenos Aires some years earlier, and the new arrivals traveled to the capitol to meet their relatives. The family was originally from the Portacomaro village of Italy.

Things went well for a few years. The Bergoglio's met up with their extended family and helped run the local business. In 1932, however, the economy went sour and they were forced to sell everything. In *El Jesuita,* Jorge Bergoglio's official biography, he recalls that all his grandfather had left was a meager two thousand pesos. His father, however, found work and the family managed to survive.

Five years after immigrating to Buenos Aires, Jorge's father and mother met. In a twist of fate, they actually met at Mass. Little did they know that their son would later go on to become the new head of the Catholic Church, which they attended faithfully. Jorge's father's name is Mario Jose Bergoglio, and his mother was Regina Maria Sivori. Unlike Jose, Regina was born in Argentina, but her family also emigrated from the northern region of Italy. They married the following year, and on the 17th of December, 1936, Jorge was born.

The couple had a total of five children, but Regina Maria was paralyzed after the fifth delivery. The children helped take care of the house, and it was during this time that Jorge learned how to cook. Regina would give the children directions in the kitchen, and they would take turns making meals. Jorge still makes his own meals at home and enjoys cooking. In his biography, Jorge recalls in his younger days how he played basketball, went to the opera, and watched classic Argentinian cinema.

Even though Jorge was born in Buenos Aires and not in his family's native homeland of Italy, as a member of an immigrant family he still had to deal with the issue of nostalgia from the older generation. He was especially close to his grandmother, who kept the cultural ties alive. Because of his multicultural heritage, Jorge knows several languages. He grew up listening to both Italian and Spanish, and developed a passion for foreign language in school.

The bright young student finished primary school at the age of thirteen, and began going to secondary school while working. His father believed that everyone must learn how to work, and that having a good work ethic was one of the most salient lessons to learn. At his father's insistence, Jorge got a job in a factory. For the first couple of years, he was in charge of cleaning and maintenance, and in the third year he moved up to an administrative position. Although he didn't necessarily see the value in the work at the time, later in life he acknowledged that he was grateful to his father for teaching him the valuable lesson of work.

The Decision to Become a Priest

At seventeen years old, Jorge was a practicing Catholic. He attended the church Portena of San Jose de Flores. One day during summer break, he planned on meeting his friends to hang out around town. At the last minute, he decided to visit the church before going. When Jorge entered the church, he knew something was different. A new priest was there, and for some reason Jorge had the strong desire to confess to him.

During the confessional, Jorge was struck by a sudden sense of awe and entered into a spiritual stupor. Years later, he tried to describe the feeling to Sergio Rubin, and said that it felt like the priest had been waiting specifically for him. Suddenly, he saw the bigger picture, and knew that God was calling to him. The experience was a deeply personal one and roused his faith in God. When he left the church, his mind was in such a turmoil that he went home instead of going out with his friends and spent a good deal of time thinking about what had happened. He decided then that he wanted to become a priest.

Jorge was still in secondary school at this time and did not tell anyone about his new conviction. However, from that day on he felt as if he belonged thoroughly and totally to God. A personal experience such as this is impossible to describe with words, but the sense that the new priest was waiting for him never left Jorge, and he still remembers the entire incident vividly.

Illness

At the age of twenty-one, the young Jorge was hospitalized with an extremely high fever. His case baffled the doctors, but eventually they diagnosed him with an extremely severe case of pneumonia. Three cysts were also detected, and they affected the upper part of his right lung. Eventually, this led to the ruined part of his lung being removed.

The whole process was painful, and the brush with death at such a young age left a distinct impression on Jorge. While in the hospital, he was comforted by a nun who helped him cope with the pain using God. During his stay, he came to realize the necessity of suffering through pain, as well as the relationship between pain and joy. He claims that the experience brought him closer to Christ and gave him valuable experience on how to hold on to religion in order to get through tough times. After the sickness had passed, Jorge emerged healthy and with a new faith in God.

Suffering is an integral part of the Christian doctrine, and the emblem of the Catholic Church is Jesus hanging on a cross while blood drips from his head, hands and feet. Since his illness, not a day had passed when Jorge has not thought of death in one way or another.

Education

Jorge finished primary school at the age of thirteen. From there, he continued on to secondary school, studying to become certified as a chemical technician. He spent many hours working in the chemistry lab. Jorge later received a master's degree in chemistry from the University of Buenos Aires. After he completed his degree program, Jorge decided to go ahead with his goal of becoming a priest and joined the Society of Jesus (or the Jesuits). The simplicity of the Jesuit lifestyle, as well as their focus on obedience and discipline appealed strongly to Jorge.

He entered the Jesuit seminary of Villa Devoto at the age of twenty-one. His family took the news that he was joining with varied reactions. Bergoglio tells his biographer that his father was happy for him, and pleased with the decision. His grandmother understood that he had been called by God, and promised him that he could come home again anytime he wished. His mother, however, was not as positive as the rest of his family. She viewed the path as a waste of Jorge's schooling and talents, and thought the decision was too hasty. She did not know, however, that Jorge had decided on his path several years before going through with joining the seminary school. The same year he entered into seminary at the Villa Devoto he became ill with his bout of pneumonia. Because of this severe health complication, Jorge was not able to participate in the missionary part of seminary. He was scheduled to go to Japan, but stayed in Buenos Aires instead.

By 1960, Jorge had earned a degree in philosophy from the Catholic University of Buenos Aires; a few years later, he became a teacher at the College of Immaculate Conception, a high school in Santa Fe. He taught literature and psychology and later taught the same classes at the College of Salvador at Buenos Aires.

As a man, Jorge has a passion for academia and study, as well as a good sense of what young adults need as students. He applied his methods of balance that he used in his own life to his teaching, making sure that he provided a solid structure to his classes but also making sufficient room for risk taking and creativity. He also struck a balance between being too distant and professional with his students, and too friendly.

While he enjoyed his teaching years, in 1967 he decided to quit teaching in order to continue his theoretical studies. He completed his studies in 1969, and finally became eligible to be ordained. Even after he became a priest, Bergoglio never stopped going to school. He spent several months abroad at a graduate school in Germany, studying philosophy and working on his dissertation. The Society of Jesus is known for its excellent schools and focus on education, and Bergoglio went on to get several more degrees.

Chapter 2: Career

Ascension Through the Ranks

Jorge Mario Bergoglio was ordained as a priest of the Catholic Church on December 13, 1969, by Ramon Jose Castellano. At thirty two years of age, he was finally beginning the career that would one day lead to him being one of the most powerful religious figures in the world.

Four years after becoming a priest, in 1973, Bergoglio was given a promotion and became the Master of Novices at a seminary in San Miguel. Staying true to his humble attitude, he admits that he made many mistakes in his early career as a priest. He told Ruben Sergio that he was put in charge of newly ordained priests at a time when he himself did not have a large amount of experience to draw on. Because of this, he had to figure things out as he went along. On a personal level, he handled his new found responsibilities by employing constant humility and by going to confession regularly. That very same year Bergoglio was also elected the provincial for the Jesuits of Argentina. He continued to serve as provincial for the next six years.

In 1992, Bergoglio became a bishop. He received the title of Auxiliary of Buenos Aires on June twenty seventh of that year. Staying true to his upward career trajectory, he was appointed the coadjutor bishop giver years later in 1997. Bergoglio remembers the moment when he first found out he was being named coadjutor bishop clearly, and recounts the experience to his biographer. The archbishop of Argentina, Quarrancino, was becoming old, and there was a lot of discussion in the Catholic community about who was going to succeed him. They decided to name a co-archbishop in advance, to rule by his side until he passed away.

One day Bergoglio was supposed to meet some of his fellow bishops to discuss the matter. It was May of 1997, and he was scheduled to meet a friend named Calabresi for lunch. When Calabresi showed up, he was carrying cake and champagne with him. Bergoglio automatically assumed that it was his friend's birthday and that he brought his own cake and champagne to celebrate with. When Bergoglio told his friend 'happy birthday', Calabresi laughed and said that the celebration was not for him. He then broke the news that Bergoglio had been chosen by the church as the new coadjutor bishop. Bergoglio was shocked at the unexpected promotion, and less than one year later he would succeed Antonio Quarrancino to be named the official archbishop of Buenos Aires.

As archbishop, Bergoglio continued to advance in the church, and took on more leadership positions. In 2005, he became the president of the Argentine Episcopal Conference, a conference that allows the bishops of Argentina to discuss relevant issues involving the Catholic Church in their country. The role of president is chosen by election, and it is a three year commitment. At the end of his initial term in 2008, he was re-elected as president again and served for three more years. It was his position as president of the Argentine Episcopal Conference that allowed Bergoglio to issue his famous apology on behalf of the Roman Catholic Church in Argentina for the wrongs committed during the Dirty War (see Chapter 3).

During his time as archbishop, Bergoglio became well-known for his sincerity and developed a reputation for his humility. He lived in a small apartment instead of the normal, more luxurious housing reserved for the bishops, and became well-known in the community because he always took the bus. He spent as much time as possible in the community and interacting with people on a personal basis. He made it a point to only travel to Rome when he was needed, and always kept his trips short so he could go back home as soon as possible.

Very soon after his promotion to archbishop, Bergoglio was promoted yet again -- this time to cardinal. In the February of 2001, he was named cardinal by Pope John Paul II. As a cardinal, Bergoglio served on several administrative congregations, including the Congregation of Divine Worship and Sacraments, the Congregation of Institutes of Consecrated Life, the Congregation of Clergy, and the Congregation of Societies of Apostolic Life.

The pope who had named Bergoglio cardinal, Pope John Paul II, died in 2005. The conclave to elect the new pope was held in April of that year. Jorge Bergoglio was one of the major contenders during the election, but Cardinal Joseph Ratzinger, a native of Germany, eventually got the vote. Rumors have circulated that before the final ballot, Bergoglio asked his fellow cardinals to vote for Ratzinger instead of him, thereby giving the position willingly to the German cardinal. While these rumors have not been confirmed, they do seem plausible due to Bergoglio's extremely humble personality.

Chapter 3: The Dirty War and Clashes With the Government

The Dirty War and Scandal

In the early 1970's, Argentina entered into a state of military dictatorship due to political and economic unrest. There was conflict throughout the country. Many people, sources say over 30,000 in number, were kidnapped, killed, or both. During such a tumultuous time, there was an excess violation of human rights. As the primary religious force in Argentina, the Catholic Church was expected to stand up to the military's treatment of the Argentine people. There were many accusations during this period of the Catholic Church not only failing to stand up for the citizens of Argentina, but acting complicit with the military in some instances.

Like many members of the church during this time, not much is known about Jorge Bergoglio's actions with regards to the government. Neither was Bergoglio free from scandal. Much later in his career, after he had already become a cardinal, accusations were brought against him by a lawyer claiming that Bergoglio had actively worked with the military in order to help them kidnap two priests whose anti-government views threatened Bergoglio's own moral stance. The two priests were named Yorio and Jalics, and they claimed that Jorge acted better than them and persecuted them because of their political stance as progressives. Since there was never any concrete evidence brought forth to confirm their story, the accusations were dropped. Those who know Bergoglio say that the accusations were nothing more than slander without any proof behind them.

Bergoglio himself did not open up about what happened during the Dirty War until his interview with biographer, Ruben Sergio. Due to all the attention and controversy that surrounded Bergoglio's actions during the time period, Sergio covered the topic thoroughly in his official biography, *El Jesuita*. In his interview, Bergoglio was well aware that during times of political unrest that the church and their leaders become more important than ever. It is the duty of the church, and its priests to make sure that they can prevent as much violation to human rights as possible. However, Bergoglio also asks people to understand that the church, because of its nature, is somewhat transcendent, and because of this sometimes the right course of action is hard to figure out.

Bergoglio recalls his experience during the early years, and says that in 1973, when the first significant shooting happened, and the events were set in motion that would eventually lead to the full blown crisis in 1976. He was a young, naive priest with only four years of experience. He had his hands full as the new Master of Novices, and many new responsibilities. At the time, he was not knowledgeable enough about the political world and the policies of the government to fully comprehend the situation.

Looking back, he can see that there were a great variety of responses by churches and priests across the country. All the priests handled the situation and the chaos a little differently, and he admits that some handled it better than others. He remembers priests and bishops who kept to their own business, and tried as hard as they could to ignore the conflict around them in order to focus solely on the work of God. However, he also knew and heard of others who rallied quickly and began to move almost immediately in defense of human rights. Still others made it seem like they were not doing anything, yet in actuality they worked extremely hard in the background to help those in need.

Bergoglio revealed specifics about his actions during the more trying times of the war, including details about Yorio and Jalics. While he did not particularly like their views, he insists that any "persecution" they experienced was imagined. He attributes their accusations of persecution to his extreme honesty that may have caused tension; however, he never wished them any will ill. Eventually, he dismissed the two priests from the order, and soon after that they were kidnapped. The priests claim that Bergoglio knew that they would be unprotected after their dismissal, and purposefully kicked them out before informing the military.

Bergoglio responded to these accusations and defended himself by revealing to Sergio the measures he took soon after the priests' kidnapping in order to find them and free them. They were eventually freed some months later and found tied up outside of Buenos Aires. Since the new information about Bergoglio's work in getting the priests' freed has surfaced, the controversy has largely died down as it became clear that, without Bergoglio's interference on their behalf, Yorio and Jalics might not have been released at all.

Bergoglio claims that he helped those in need in a more behind the scenes fashion whenever he could. He recalls hiding refugees in the parish church, and even disguising one man in his priest clothing and giving him his own id in order to smuggle him out of the country. Critics of Bergoglio say that he acted cowardly for not opening up sooner about his actions during the Dirty War. Those who know Bergoglio defend him by saying that his extremely humble, and private nature is the reason for the lack of interaction with the media about the issue.

Recognizing that the people of Argentina were unsatisfied by the work of the Catholic Church during the conflict, under Bergoglio's presidency, the bishops of Argentina issued a formal, collective apology in October of 2012. After Bergoglio's election to pope, the scandal about his actions during the Dirty War has been brought back to the table. The Vatican, however, claims it is old news.

Clashes with the Argentine Government

Jorge Bergoglio became well-known for his conflicts with both the past president of Argentina, Nestor Kirchner, as well as his wife (and later successor) Christina Fernandez de Kirchner. The problems began in 2004, when then-president Nestor Kirchner attended a mass on a national holiday. The sermon was given by Bergoglio, then a cardinal, and he talked about the need to get rid of intolerance in the government. Kirchner was positive that the comments were directed at him, and took great offense to the sermon. From that point on, he attended mass elsewhere.

Later, when Bergoglio was asked by reporters about the passages, and if they did, in fact, refer to the president's actions in the government, Bergoglio remained vague, saying only that the comments were aimed at all the Argentine people, president Kirchner included. Nestor Kirchner passed away in 2010, leaving the country to his wife, Christiana Fernandez de Kirchner.

In 2010, the same year as her husband's death, Christina Fernandez passed a law that legalized same-sex marriage. The bill was widely regarded as a movement forward within the country, as the majority of Argentinians were in favor of its passage. However, as a traditional Catholic, Bergoglio vehemently opposed the bill. According to the New York Times, Bergoglio called the bill a "destructive attack on God's plan." The clashes with the Argentine government only continued as Christina Fernandez put forth bills that would legalize the adoption of children by same sex couples, which Bergoglio called "discrimination against children." Bergoglio also publicly opposed bills that would offer free contraception for the women of Argentina.

After Bergoglio's election to pope, he met with Christina Fernandez in an effort to improve relations. She sent him a letter offering congratulations, and hopes to work with him on improving Argentina's relations worldwide.

Chapter 4: Beliefs

A Quick Breakdown

Abortion - strongly against abortion, believes life begins at conception

Euthanasia - strongly against euthanasia, calls it a "crime against life"

Death Penalty - strongly against the death penalty

Same sex marriage - strongly against same sex marriage, defies God's natural order

Same sex adoption - strongly against

Contraceptives - against the use of contraceptives

Sex education - supports sex education

Poverty - believes strongly in helping the poor

Celibacy - against the removal of celibacy in the Church

State of the Catholic Church - needs to focus on pastoral work and expansion

Stance on Key Issues

Pro-Life: Abortion, Euthanasia and the Death Penalty

On issues regarding life, the new Pope Francis consistently chooses stances that preserve and protect life, not matter what the form. These are traditional stances held by the Catholic Church and were also held by the previous Pope Benedict XVI. The reason Bergoglio takes this traditional stance is because he believes that life should be valued above all else. He believes that every person has the right to be born, live a fulfilled life, and die a natural death.

In *El Jesuita,* he makes it clear that he believes life begins at contraception. He believes that life from conception is a scientific way of life, despite the scientific controversy surrounding the issue. The reason for this is that the newly made cells already contain the entire genetic code needed for life to form. Because of this, even if the cells are not a fetus, he still considers them human and believes that they deserve all the rights a child or adult human has. From the moment those cells are created with that genetic blueprint, Bergoglio considers them to be alive. When a fetus is aborted, the fundamental right to live is taken away from them.

Bergoglio, however, recognizes that there are issues that need to be addressed, not just by the Catholic Church but by society and government as a whole, for abortions to no longer be needed. He sympathizes with women who have chosen to get abortions because of pressure, whether professional or personal. He believes that women who are considering getting abortions need to be cared for with loving kindness during pregnancy. They need the support of the church, a priest, or even their family, in order to appreciate the gift of life they have been given. Bergoglio believes this can only happen if the judgment and stigmas surrounding these women can be overcome, and if society is willing to take an active role in helping solve the issue.

His biography gives several other things that Bergoglio believes need to be changed in society for abortions to no longer be necessary. One of these is providing sufficient physical care for the mother during the pregnancy, as well as physical and emotional care after the baby is born. The time right after a child is born is stressful for both mother and child, and many countries do not give women enough time off from work or make it hard to find affordable child care.

All of these issues contribute to reason why women feel the need to get abortions in the first place, and if society treated women with this in mind and provided adequate support, then Bergoglio believes women would not resort to getting an abortion. He has talked to many women personally who have had abortions performed, and says that all of them regretted it later and considered the act as murdering their own child. He hates to see women go through such pain, and mourns for children that they have lost.

In keeping with his strictly pro-life stance, Pope Francis has also been adamant about the immorality of euthanasia and the death sentence. He believes that, in a traditional family structure, the elderly are not discarded or hidden away in a home like so many are today. Since modern culture has increasingly focused on the young, he believes that the elderly have been set aside. As a result, families don't take the time and effort to care for their elders, and resort to euthanasia rather than deal with the time commitment and monetary support.

Once again, in his biography Bergoglio defends his stance on euthanasia by saying that he values life above all else. Just as he believes that a baby has the right to live a healthy, fulfilled life, he also believes that the elderly have the right to a natural death. Allowing the elders of society to die with their families and without medication, to Bergoglio, means that they died with dignity.

Because of Bergoglio's traditional, pro-life stance, he has drawn much criticism from the media not only for his conservatism, but also for the extremely strong expression of his beliefs on these controversial issues. In a speech, he famously compared legalizing abortion to legalizing the death penalty, and called euthanasia a "crime against life", even in cases of assisted suicide.

Same Sex Relations: Marriage, Adoption and the Treatment of Gays

Bergoglio strongly opposes homosexuality on the ground that it is wholly unnatural and goes against God's plan. Although he does not agree with homosexuality, he believes it is a sin to treat any person differently because of their orientation. He thinks that the church is too exclusive, that everybody has their own sins, and that homosexuals are people just like everybody else.

Despite his strong belief that homosexuals should not be discriminated against, however, his outspoken opinion about the issue, as well as his vocal opposition of the Argentine government legalizing same sex marriage, has led to a host of criticism. Catholic Online also writes that Bergoglio is against the adoption of children by homosexual couples, citing it as a "form of discrimination against children". Many of his critics find this point of view ironic, considering all the recent political scandal involving child abuse in the Catholic Church.

Sexuality: Contraception and Sex Education

Bergoglio keeps with the traditional views of the Catholic Church with regards to contraception, although he is much less outspoken about the issue than others such as abortion and euthanasia. However, he did oppose the legislation put forth by the Argentine government that would offer free contraception to all Argentine citizens.

Although some Catholics may be against sex education, Bergoglio assured his biographer that he believes differently. Personally, Bergoglio believes that members of the church, especially young boys, should be taught about sex and sexuality. He believes that it should be done gradually, however, with multiple education classes for different stages of development. The only issue he has with sex education classes is that he feels they can become degrading to the students if they are not conducted properly.

Economics: Poverty, Work and Modern-day Slavery

Perhaps the most defining characteristic of Jorge Mario Bergoglio is his deep love and sympathy for the poor and impoverished of society. Just as Jesus spent most of his time with beggars, cripples, and other underprivileged, so too does Bergoglio place enormous emphasis on helping the lower classes. It is his great passion for the poor that defines his life and is one of the reasons he took a vow of poverty when he entered the priesthood.

Because of his humble background as the son of an immigrant worker, Bergoglio has an immense respect for the working class. In his biography, he reveals that he is sympathetic towards the impoverished and those without jobs. He says that, in his experience, most of the people who are unemployed are not in that situation willingly. They want more than anything to work, to prove themselves, to make something of their lives and provide for their families. Work, he emphasizes, is dignity, and without a good work ethic it is hard to live a fulfilled life.

He places enormous importance on the value of work, and goes so far as to say that the governments should foster a culture of work and not one of giving. Of course, states of emergency are an exception to this. Bergoglio worries that hard work has, in many parts of the world but especially in the more wealthy countries, been replaced by a culture of instant gratification. Many parents do not teach their children the value of hard work, creating adults who may not know how to contribute to society or lead fulfilled lives. Much of his personal belief about work and poverty were shaped by his father, Jose Mario Bergoglio, an immigrant who came to Buenos Aires with nothing and created a life for himself. His father was the one who taught him how to work at a young age, and those lessons have stayed with Bergoglio throughout his adult life.

Bergoglio acknowledges that there are problems in the modern world that lead to poverty. The main issue, especially in countries like Argentina that are depressed economically, is that there simply not enough jobs to go around. On the other hand, many people who are career obsessed suffer from over work. Afraid that if they do not work hard enough, or put in enough extra time, they will lose their jobs, they put in countless hours off the clock. This takes valuable time away from leisure and family, which Bergoglio views as just as important as a good work life.

He emphasizes the importance of being able to balance the work life and home life in a healthy manner, and also worries that Sunday as a day of rest has largely gone out of the culture because people are expected to work that day. He attributes over work to a huge host of problems in society, and believes that when a family reaches the point where the parents do not even have enough time to play with their children that they cannot be living a fulfilled life. In place of a life of meaning, they have become slaves to consumerism and the demands and expectations of society.

While slavery does not exist today in exactly the same way as it did in the Old Testament, Bergoglio believes that slavery still exists in the modern world; although he admits that it takes on more subtle forms and is not as easily recognizable. The modern forms of slavery, he insists, are just as cruel and unfair as the previous ways of buying, selling, and shipping slaves - they just are not as obvious.

He points to Bolivians that work in exploitive factory conditions, and the hundreds of sweatshops that exist around the world. In places like this, people are forced to work long, exhausting hours for little reward and, in some cases, not even enough to survive on. In his mind, this is absolutely a kind of slavery. The impoverished in this instance are trapped by their position. They must make a living somehow, and the factories and sweatshops exploit them because of their vulnerability, keeping them trapped in a state of dependence.

He also points out that the sex trade is responsible for numerous instances of modern day slavery. Women are kidnapped or sold as prostitutes and sometimes even as "wives". Young children often meet this fate, as well. Those brought into the sex trade often have no choice about their fate, and no way to escape it. Bergoglio wants to end slavery, in any form, and acts as a champion of the poor.

Hypocrisy and Baptism

Other than Bergoglio's deep sympathy for the impoverished, his hatred of what he calls leading a "double life" is one of the things that defines his lifestyle and method as a priest the most. He had a strong dislike for any that lead dishonest lives but is especially harsh on his fellow religious leaders. Bergoglio is well known for publicly chastising the priests of his order, and in one speech he accused church administrators and officials for failing to follow in Jesus' footsteps. He reminded them that Jesus spent most of his time in the slums, with beggars and prostitutes, instead of attending parties and talking to politicians.

In his own life, he makes sure to practice what he preaches. His first few days as the newly anointed pope prove that. Every decision that he makes, he double checks against his set of beliefs to make perfectly sure that he does not commit hypocrisy with his actions. He talks about never following his first hunch on how to act in any given situation because he believes it is usually not the right course of action.

Bergoglio has also become famous throughout the clerical society for accusing priests who refuse to baptize children who were born out of wedlock of hypocrisy. Keeping with his stance of sympathy for women who end up pregnant and alone, he praises their courage for choosing not to get an abortion. Because of this, he thinks it is abhorrent that a single woman must try several different parishes before they can find one who will baptize their child. Because of this reluctance to baptize those who are willing, Bergoglio thinks that the church has taken an exclusive stance on how they interact with the world and local communities. He believes that the church should be more open and accepting rather than judgmental and that everyone should be treated with an equal amount of respect and love.

Chapter 5: Opinions on the Catholic Church

Status of the Church Worldwide

The new Pope Francis recognizes that the Catholic Church is in different places all across the world and that each country or continent does not necessarily need to follow the same approach with regards to leadership. In his biography, he describes Europe's Catholic Church to be in a state of crisis, while Africa and Asia are busy expanding rapidly due to population booms and an increase in religion. In the United States, there are so many varieties that it is difficult to take a generalized approach.

One thing that Bergoglio is adamant about, however, is the need of the church to focus on expansion and move in a more pastoral direction. He does not believe that churches should enclose themselves inside their own small communities, because that is like a person living with a closed mind. Instead, the church needs to focus on expanding and growing. If not, the church will only focus on itself and won't take the time or effort to connect with surrounding communities. The result of this is that churches become increasingly exclusive and paranoid. One change that Bergoglio believes would help the Catholic Church grow would be to alter the structure of the church to put the focus back onto missionary work as well as local outreach.

Priests

The main thing Bergoglio notices about priests is their tendency to become administrators instead of priests. He believes that they need to be more personal and avoid the temptation to assume only a leadership role. He has seen many priests distance themselves from their congregations, when they should instead to striving to connect with them on a deeper, more personal level. Not only that, but they should actively go out and seek new members as well as help the people in the community. This hands on, personal approach is what has shaped the new Pope Francis' entire career and made him famous for his conversational, one on one style sermons.

He is adamant that even those who have high positions in the church should not forget about the basic needs of their flock. Just because they are higher up on the chain doesn't mean that they should be allowed to separate themselves from the people they are teaching, or that they are any better than them. Bergoglio uses Cardinal Casaroli as an example of this. Casaroli was promoted to be the Secretary of State of the Vatican, but even after his promotion he continued to visit a local juvenile prison every weekend. Bergoglio looks up to Cardinal Casaroli as an example, and believes that more priests should learn from his behavior and make an effort to engage with their communities using similar tactics.

Bergoglio has kept his actions in line with his beliefs after assuming the new position of pope. He has made special efforts to keep himself ingrained in the culture of the church by keeping his simplistic lifestyle and refusing many of the luxurious perks that traditionally come with the title.

Celibacy and Sex Scandals

The past decade has seen the Catholic Church become torn apart from the inside due to numerous sex scandals involving priests and the abuse of young children, particularly boys. Many critics of the church speculate that the scandals are a direct result of the strict policy of celibacy for the priests and administrators of the church.

Pope Francis talks to his biographer about his opinion on the vow of celibacy that all priests are required to take, and discusses whether or not getting rid of the policy would help the current crisis that the church is facing. Bergoglio reveals that he, personally, does not believe that the scandals are caused by the vow of celibacy. He also does not believe that the Catholic Church would choose to get rid of the policy because of them. In this respect, he openly agrees with the late Pope Benedict XVI on the issue.

Bergoglio believes that pedophilia is not the result of celibacy, but rather that people either have the perversion or they don't. He gives a statistic to defend his position, saying that seventy percent of cases involving pedophilia occur in the family or neighborhood environment. Many young children, and boys, and abused by their fathers, uncles, and even grandparents. Therefore, he believes that it is hard to make a case for pedophilia as the result of celibacy because it obviously exists outside of the church in large numbers and in most cases does not involve those who have taken a vow.

If anything, he believes that the church should be more selective about who should be allowed to enter the priesthood in the first place and says that would go a long way in solving the problem of the recent scandals. He thinks that tests should be used to rigorously determine whether or not someone is psychologically sound enough to join the order, and to make sure that any new priests who enter into the Catholic Church do not have any major perversions.

Bergoglio defends celibacy as a choice, saying it is similar to the vow of poverty he took when he joined the Society of Jesus. Still, he admits that it is common for those who have taken a vow of celibacy, especially those who joined the order at a young age, to fall in love. In cases such as these, he recommends giving up the priesthood if it is genuine love and not merely being mistaken for lust. This prevents the temptation of living a double live and committing the sin of hypocrisy. He knows not everyone is perfect, but stoutly believes that people should choose to either give up their vocation or to remain completely celibate in order to live honest lives.

There are also those who want to lift the policy of celibacy because of the recent shortage of priests in the Catholic Church. While Bergoglio admits that the church might eventually change their stance on celibacy, he doesn't think it will be because of the priest shortage. Rather, it would have to come about as the result of a larger cultural shift. And while lifting the policy might result in more priests, it would also attract more people who are not as serious about the vocation. In the end, lifting the policy might even result in more scandals.

Fear and Guilt in the Church

It is a well-known fact that many priests give what are aptly named "fire and brimstone" sermons, using the threat of hell and eternal damnation in order to get their audience to submit to and fear God. The Catholic Church is no exception to these sorts of tactics. While some in the Catholic Church are fine with this style of preaching, and even find it invigorating, there are others who believe that it is an archaic and harmful way to preach the gospel.

Bergoglio does not believe in using fear as a means of fueling faith. In fact, he believes just the opposite. He would much rather preach the gospel using love and joy to bring people closer together, and believes that the message of love is much more similar to the preaching of Jesus. He believes that if Jesus were alive in modern times he would be using love and acceptance instead of fear to preach the gospel and bring new members to the church.

The most important thing for Bergoglio is his personal relationship with God, and he thinks that should be the most important priority for all practicing Catholics. Highly negative emotions such as fear serve to hinder relationships and stall growth. Of course, some fear is necessary in order to truly comprehend God, but Bergoglio insists that a faith motivated by fear is not a healthy way to establish a loving relationship. As he says in his biography - "positive unites, while negative divides".

Another criticism of the church that is widespread is the idea that religion guilts people into joining, and causes them to experience severely agonized emotions over normal, human reactions to the world. To Bergoglio, this is not the case at all. Taking a unique point of view on the issue, he sees being aware of one's sins as a positive thing, because along with that awareness comes the knowledge that Jesus died to save humanity. While fear is a purely negative tactic that Bergoglio would rather not use in his sermons, he views the emotion of guilt and the personal awareness of sins as an opportunity for growth and development. To him, this awareness has the ability to connect people to each other, and also to God.

Catholicism in the Modern Era

A problem being recognized by the religious all over the world is the "consumerism" of religion. The Catholic Church is no exception to this phenomenon, and many wonder how the church will change in order to keep up with the times. As the Catholic Church sticks to traditional stances and resists the more liberal changes occurring in many first world countries, some wonder if people will stick with the religion when it preaches unpopular messages.

Even within Catholicism, there is a tendency to pick and choose churches, as well as priests, as one would choose a product. Possible church-goers weigh the pros and cons in order to decide which religion, church, or priest is best for them. Bergoglio recognizes that this is a problem, but stresses that the only people who get hurt by this process are the ones who get caught up in it. The most important thing, to Bergoglio, is a person's one on one relationship with God. When the religious become overly engaged in activities like finding the perfect church or the perfect priest, he believes that it detracts from the religious experience. This sort of consumerism with regards to religion can quickly cheapen the deep spiritual connection that is the defining aspect of religion.

While he does not wish to warn people away from finding the best churches or priests, he urges the religious not to get too caught up in the spectacle and forget the heart of religion. No matter where someone goes to church, or whose sermon they listen to, Bergoglio insists that it is the personal relationship with The Lord that is truly important.

Chapter 6: Pope Francis I

His Election to Pope

After the sudden resignation of Pope Benedict XVI due to health reasons, the Catholic Church was in turmoil. The conclave to elect the two hundred and sixty-sixth pope began on the twelfth of March. There was much speculation about who was going to be elected.

Many were sure that the conclave would elect a young pope with enough energy to revive the Catholic Church after the numerous scandals and criticisms of recent years. A young pope, analysts believed, would live long enough to see the Catholic Church stabilized and rebuilt. Many cardinals before the conclave began reported that they would not want to elect any one older than seventy years old in order to avoid another sudden resignation due to aging. At seventy six years old, Jorge Bergoglio was not even on the radar. Analysts gave him odds of winning ranging from twenty five to one, to thirty three to one.

Before the conclave began, two main camps began to emerge. One camp wanted to keep the papacy in Europe, and there was a movement to elect an Italian pope in particular. The second camp wanted to move away from Europe in order to focus on the rising Catholic numbers in other nations. Because Latin Americans count for over forty percent of the Church's members, many thought that a pope from Latin America would be welcome; however, there was no real guarantee that such a pope would be elected.

In order to be elected pope, a single candidate must claim at least two thirds of the majority. Out of one hundred and fifteen seats, at least seventy seven are needed to win. All cardinals under the age of eighty are eligible to be elected the next pope, and it is traditional for all those eligible to travel to the Vatican City a week before the conclave begins in order to foster discussion and friendship.

Because of the state of turmoil produced by the resignation of Pope Benedict XVI, the two hundred and sixty sixth conclave was expected to be an especially long one. However, the election was over surprisingly quickly, lasting for only five rounds of ballots. The traditional white smoke rose at 7:06 pm in the evening on March 13, 2013, and bells were rung all over the city to announce the new pope.

Bergoglio's election surprised many, if not all, of those waiting for news. Since he had not even been considered a viable candidate, many did not even know his name. Curiosity began to abound about how he came out of seemingly nowhere in order to win the papal seat. Apparently, during the first round of ballots, his name came up more times than anyone expected. This caused attention to be drawn to him within the conclave, and he began to be seen as a possible candidate. Reports say that Bergoglio's constant humility during the discussions eventually caused others to take notice, and over the course of the five ballots, Bergoglio's name began gaining more and more votes.

Bergoglio seemed as shocked as everyone else by the decision of the conclave, and when he addressed the thousands of watchers from the balcony on St. Peter's square, he reportedly acted shy. He gave the traditional speech but began with the humble opening of "brothers and sisters" immediately fostering a sense of equality and familiarity with the people watching around the world.

Over the next few days, the new Pope Francis' actions were dissected closely, and he came to be admired for his simplistic lifestyle and willingness to bend or even break tradition. Because of the unprecedented situation of having both a retired pope and an active pope, there was some worry that there would be clashes of power between Benedict XVI and Francis. However, Pope Francis called Benedict soon after he was elected, and reportedly visited him in order to establish a friendly relation.

World Wide Response

Among the most enthusiastic about the election of the new Pope Francis are the Latin Americans, who make up over forty percent of the world's practicing Catholics. Although they did not expect to have a Latin American pope, they are excited about finally gaining significant representation in the hierarchy of the Catholic Church. As archbishop of Buenos Aires, Jorge Bergoglio was well loved by the Catholic population of Argentina, and there are many people who have personal stories of encounters with him both before and during his career.

Although Bergoglio has had rocky relations with the past two presidents of Argentina, they appear to have put their differences aside after the election. Christina Fernandez de Kirchner, the current president of Argentina, has reportedly met with the new Pope Francis in order to congratulate him as well as work with him on improving Argentine relations throughout the world. Those from Argentina view the election as a chance to put their country back on the radar and gain political status worldwide.

The United States has also had a positive response to the election of the new pope, and is hopeful about how he will expand the church in the future. Much of Europe was pleased with Pope Francis, but there was a group of Italians in particular who are a bit disgruntled by the conclave's choice. After Pope Benedict XVI's resignation, there was a growing movement in Italy that wanted to bring the papacy back to its original roots and elect a highly traditional Italian as pope. Because the last two popes, Pope John Paul II and Pope Benedict XVI, were not Italian, many expected the church to come back home.

After the election of Pope Francis from Argentina, many analysts speculate about whether or not an Italian will again be elected pope. Many believe that as Catholic membership increases in other parts of the world, that the likelihood of having another Italian pope will decline. They cite Bergoglio's surprising election as evidence that the Catholic Church is moving away from Europe. As new pope, Francis' personal emphasis on missionary work and outreach will only further the Church's growth outside of Europe. In the early 1900's, over two thirds of the Catholic population was centered in Europe. During the past century, however, the number of European Catholics and non-European has switched, leaving just a quarter of the world's Catholic population in Europe.

As archbishop, Bergoglio reportedly had good relations with other religious factions, including the Jewish and Islamic populations. The leaders of these religions are hopeful that the good relations will continue in the future, and are excited about the humility of the Pope Francis.

Perhaps the main group who is disappointed in the election of the pope is the secular groups around the world. As the percentage of non-religious continues to rise in many countries, such as the United States, there was hope that the new pope would be able to make more liberal allowances on key issues such as abortion and same-sex marriage.

Over all, the Pope Francis' lifestyle of humility has earned him the love and respect of millions around the world. Many stories of his refusal to ride in the papal limousine, his insistence that he cooks his own meals and his passion for the lower classes have already circulated the web and paved the way for his years as pope.

Breaking Tradition - Pope Francis' Humility

While Jorge Bergoglio holds traditional stances on key issues such as abortion and same sex marriage, in many ways he breaks the traditions of the Catholic Church. He is already becoming known as a pope who is bringing many firsts into the papal see. Not only is he the first pope to be elected from the Americas, but he is also the first to be elected from the Southern Hemisphere. He is the first Jesuit, and also the first trained chemist to become pope.

Even as his first few days as pope, Francis has been bending the traditional pomp and circumstance of the Vatican. After he was elected, he greeted the world for the first time while wearing unadorned white robes instead of the red of previous popes. In addition, he refused to stand on a platform above the other cardinals when he gave his speech. He began his speech with the casual greeting of "brothers and sisters", a clear sign that he was not planning on following the formality of his predecessors. The previous popes have always given their blessing to the masses during their first speech as pope; using his humility to change the tables, the new Pope Francis instead asked the people to pray for him.

Before elected pope, he had a reputation for not taking advantage of the luxuries the Vatican had to offer, and became famous for riding the bus and living in a small apartment. Since becoming pope, Francis has continued to live a simple lifestyle and has made efforts to step outside the zone that the Catholic Church traditionally occupies. He has received positive attention, in one example, for blessing a Seeing Eye dog that was unexpectedly at his first sermon. Another instance that has made him famous is his visit to a hospital in Argentina as archbishop of Buenos Aires. During the visit, he washed the feet of twelve AIDS patients who were experiencing severe complications due to their illness. He kissed their feet after washing them, and told his fellow priests that society often forgets "the sick and the poor".

The differences between the previous Pope Benedict XVI and the newly elected Pope Francis are remarkably distinct. While Benedict was primarily interested in academia, and had a lofty style of speech, Pope Francis puts his emphasis on pastoral work and is known for his conversational and easy to understand speeches.

Chapter 7: Criticisms and the Future of the Catholic Church

Criticisms of the New Pope

Although the general reaction to Jorge Bergoglio's election as Pope Francis has been positive, he still has some critics who worry that he will be incapable of leading the Catholic Church forward. Much of his media criticism has been centered on his actions during the seventies and the scandal that arose during the Dirty War. Even if his actions were not worth accusing, his extreme humility and media shy nature caused problems in resolving the issue. He did not open up about his actions until 2010 when he granted an interview with his biographer, Ruben Sergio. Many claim that he waited too long to speak to the media about the Dirty War and that he failed to take action.

In other matters, however, especially in his dealings with the Argentine government and his constant clashes with presidents Nestor Kirchner and Christina Fernandez de Kirchner, many accuse him to being too direct and harsh. Especially in the early 2000's, when Argentina was experiencing economic problems, he was so outspoken on issues regarding the impoverished that he became overly critical of those in power. While many admired Bergoglio's actions as archbishop and cardinal of Argentina and his willingness to challenge authority, others tended to view his manner as too harsh.

Bergoglio's reputation as a homebody also has some critics worried. Before elected pope, Bergoglio always kept his visits to Rome short and relatively rare. In comparison to past popes, such as John Paul II, who constantly made an effort to evangelize by traveling the world, Bergoglio has kept under the radar. He is so connected to his homeland that he might negatively influence Catholicism in other countries by putting too much emphasis on his home land.

Those who wanted a more liberal pope are also highly critical of Bergoglio as Pope Francis. Many progressive Catholics have been calling for reform on key issues for years, and were hoping that the predecessor of Pope Benedict XVI would help modernize the Catholic Church with regards to women's rights and same sex marriage.

The Future of Francis and the Catholic Church

While it would not be possible for one man to single handedly fix all the issues present in the modern day Catholic Church, there are high hopes that the new pope will lead the Church in the right direction. Under his leadership, the church will most likely place a new interest in evangelism and helping the poor. His example as an extremely humble servant of God might improve the reputation of the Vatican worldwide, and perhaps new priests would take after his actions.

As the first Jesuit and the first pope from the Americas, many analysts believe that his election as pope signals a new age for the Catholic Church - one that is moving away from the traditional European seat of power and into countries such as Latin America and Asia. As the Church moves away from its western roots, a new era might well be on its way in which pastoral work and quiet academic study could be more valuable than the luxuriousness of the Vatican.

When Francis of Assisi first took his vow of poverty as a result of the opulence of wealth surrounding him, he made enormous wages across the culture of Catholicism. He became a saint for his return to the pastoral roots of Christianity and is a well-loved religious figure to this day. As the first pope to take the name Francis, the humble man from an immigrant family could very well make the same sort of waves across the culture of the modern day church.

Although Bergoglio breaks with tradition in some respects, and will undoubtedly put a new focus on the Catholic Church's aims, he is still conservative. Those who have been calling for more liberal reform in the church in response to the changing morality of the first world will most likely be disappointed by Pope Francis' staunch conservative views. While Francis may move the church forward with regards to bringing in more Latin American influence, there are many who believe that the church will not survive unless it becomes much more liberal and is willing to work with governments instead of against them on issues such as women's rights, same sex marriage and abortion.

In the end, the election of Bergoglio as Pope Francis will most likely have both positive and negative effects on the Catholic Church. By going back to the roots of Christianity, the Church will gain more respect and admiration in the world wide community. However, by refusing to keep up with the times and sticking with the Church's traditional stance on issues, the Catholic Church may continue to stagnate despite the best efforts of its administrators. Of course, as no one was able to predict either the resignation of Pope Benedict XVI or the election of Pope Francis, the future of the Catholic Church remains full of mystery and change.

Chapter 8: A Short History Lesson

The Modern Catholic Church

Even though the Catholic Church is one of the older religious societies, it nevertheless remains a relevant, powerful force in the modern times. The Catholic Church had extremely humble beginnings, rising out from the Christian religion spread by Peter after Jesus' lifetime. Eventually, the Catholic Church was born out of the Roman Empire when the Roman emperor Constantine named Christianity the official religion in order to unify his sprawling empire. From that point on, the Catholic Church only continued to grow larger and gain more and more influence in the western world. Although they clashed heavily with the pagan worshippers in Rome, the Islamic religion that arose from the prophet Mohammad, and even itself when it grew too large, it remained the dominant religion of the western civilization.

In medieval Europe, the Catholic Church and the Vatican held more power than many governments, and even the Kings were required to yield to the pope, the infallible head of the Catholic Church. In the thirteenth century, smaller divisions of the Church began to appear, including the Franciscan Order of Friars created by Francis of Assisi, who is the namesake of the new Pope Francis.

In the modern era, Catholicism has been criticized for holding on to antiquated and out dated beliefs and traditions. As a response, the Church has put more focus on evangelism. Pope John Paul II, who named Jorge Bergoglio Cardinal, made a significant effort to revive the Catholic Church in the modern age; however, the Church's revival efforts have been hindered by many problems in recent times.

Among the main issues that plague the Church are controversies involving the changing morals of sexuality and gender. The Catholic Church is traditionally against homosexuality, sex before marriage, and the use of contraception. In addition, the hierarchy of the Church is comprised of men exclusively holding the positions of power. Women can join the ranks of the Church as nuns or sisters, but are not permitted to hold any positions of authority.

In a world where the tides are changing to allow women equal rights with men, homosexuals the right to marry, and where it has become common place to engage in sexual relations before marriage, the number of practicing Catholics, as well as new priests entering the order, has dropped.

The Church has also been faced with numerous problems because of continual sex scandals, usually involving priests and young boys. Not only were the scandals spread virally through the rise of social media use and readily available news, but the Church also drew heavy criticism for trying to ignore the issues. In the face of these mounting problems, the Church has elected a man of simplicity and humility to restore their respect in the eyes of the world.

The Society of Jesus

As the first Jesuit ever to attain the title of pope, the new Pope Francis has broken all precedent and redefined not only the Jesuit order but also the Catholic Church as a whole. To understand the significance of a pope from the Society of Jesus, it is necessary to take a quick peek into the history of the order.

The Society of Jesus was founded by Saint Ignatius Loyola in the mid 1500's. Loyola did not originally intend on creating a religious order, but only wanted to reform his own personal actions. Looking at the state of the Catholic Church, he noticed that many priests were not following the teachings of Jesus, and were in some cases acting contrary to their original roots. Loyola decided to reform his own actions in order to better imitate the actions of Jesus, and in doing so become closer to God and his word. He believed that the Catholic Church had become too corrupt and extravagant, and made it his mission to live a more simple religious life.

Over the years, he gained some fame for his reform and others began following his example. Eventually, his followers became so numerous that Loyola needed to create an official order. He spent the last years of his life testing rules and writing the Constitutions of what he named the Society of Jesus. Because of the focus of the Society on imitating Christ, the creation of the Constitutions was slow.

Pope Francis appears to be following in Loyola's footsteps, as he has been slow to make changes to the church in his first few days as Pope. It is traditional for the new pope to quickly rearrange positions and make new appointments, but Francis has purposefully refrained from making any quick decisions about how the church is to be reorganized.

The early Society of Jesus placed a strong emphasis on missionary work and the pastoral expansion of the church, both locally and abroad. The Society was responsible for sending missionaries into many non-Christian countries including India, Japan, and the South Americas. As a South American Jesuit, Bergoglio also places a strong emphasis on missionary work and outreach and is expected to take the Catholic Church in a more pastoral direction.

To become a Jesuit priest, members must study for over a decade. It is also necessary to take two month long retreats in which the priests cultivate their self-discipline and faith in isolation. As the first pope who is trained in chemistry, Bergoglio shows that he has a strong love for academia. He is also well trained in philosophy, literature, psychology and theology.

Over the years after the Society of Jesus was established, the order became known for its focus on academia, missionary work and expansion, as well as the vow of poverty and simplistic lifestyle. Because of this, it is not common for members of the Society of Jesus to seek out positions of power and authority within the larger Catholic hierarchy. Since Pope Francis' election as pope, many have speculated that, in order to have accepted the position, that he experienced a strong call to service. Those who know Bergoglio do not believe that he took the position out of a quest for authority, but think he truly believed he needed to accept the position.

Behind the Name: Francis of Assisi

As the first of his name, Pope Francis has made a powerful statement about how he intends to lead the Catholic Church. Although when he announced his new name, there was some confusion about whether it was referring to Saint Francis of Assisi, famous for his life style of humility and poverty, or Xavier Francis, a famous Jesuit missionary who focused on evangelism and also helped found the Society of Jesus, Bergoglio clarified in his first meeting with the media that he was indeed referring to the Saint Francis of Assisi.

Saint Francis of Assisi lived during the late 1100's and died in the year 1226. His father was a wealthy merchant cloth trader, and his mother belonged to family of noble blood. The story of Francis says that, in his youth, Francis was famous for chasing worldly goods and pleasures and that he made the most of his wealthy status. When he was still a young man, however, Francis entered into a small war and was taken captive by the enemies of Assisi. His imprisonment greatly affected him, as well as an illness that left him near death. When Francis was released, he continued in a military career, however, he was plagued by strange dreams that eventually compelled him to go back to him home town of Assisi and live as a beggar.

Francis became extremely religious, giving up all his gold and even his inheritance gladly. He traveled across the country, preaching to small villages and working wherever he could. Eventually, he joined the Catholic Church and lived out the rest of his life in service of the Church. During the last years of his life, Francis founded the Franciscan Order of Friars, who held to the ideals of helping the poor and living a simple, monk-like existence. Before he died, Francis was named a saint by Cardinal Ugolino, and he later became known as the patron saint of animals. There are many tales of Francis preaching to the local animals or calming wild beasts.

The name Francis has become associated wholly with sincerity, simplicity, and humility. In choosing the papal name Francis, Bergoglio is sending a message that humility and not extravagance is what the Church should stand for. In his first meeting with the press, Bergoglio gave some more details about how he chose the name. When it became clear that he had a good chance of being chosen, one of his fellow cardinals reminded him not to forget the poor. When Bergoglio heard this, he immediately thought of Saint Francis, who was known for his love of peace and goodwill towards the impoverished.

Bibliography

Books

A History of the Society of Jesus by William V. Bangert
El Jesuita, The official biography by Ruben Sergio
The Catholic Church: A Short History by Hans Kung

News Articles

http://www.nydailynews.com/news/world/pope-francis-humble-affable-servant-article-1.1288163
http://visnews-en.blogspot.com/2013/03/biography-who-is-jorge-mario-bergoglio.html
http://www.catholicherald.co.uk/news/2013/03/13/cardinal-bergoglio-profile/
http://my.chicagotribune.com/#section/-1/article/p2p-74812678/
http://www.nytimes.com/2013/03/15/world/europe/pope-francis.html?ref=francisi&_r=0

http://www.catholicnews.com/jpii/cardinals/0
501841.htm

http://www.catholic.org/hf/faith/story.php?id
=50111

http://www.jesuit.org/2013/03/13/jesuit-
argentine-cardinal-jesuit-bergoglio-
elected-pope-takes-name-francis-i/

http://www.cbsnews.com/8301-202_162-
57574147/jorge-bergoglio-who-is-the-
new-pope/

http://www.usatoday.com/story/news/world
/2013/03/13/how-will-francis-lead-his-
church/1986363/

http://www.usatoday.com/story/news/world
/2013/03/13/why-named-francis-
assisi/1986017/

http://www.cnn.com/2013/03/13/world/euro
pe/vatican-pope-bergoglio-profile

http://www.30giorni.it/articoli_id_16457_l3.ht
m

http://www.lanacion.com.ar/604859-el-
mensaje-de-la-iglesia-era-para-kirchner

http://www.nytimes.com/2010/07/14/world/
americas/14argentina.html?_r=1&

http://www.lifewithdogs.tv/2013/03/pope-
francis-makes-exception-to-bless-guide-
dog/

http://www.reuters.com/article/2013/03/14/u
s-pope-bergoglio-
idUSBRE92D16J20130314

http://www.religionnews.com/2013/03/13/je
ws-worldwide-see-an-ally-in-pope-
francis/

http://www.lifenews.com/2013/03/13/cardina
l-jorge-mario-bergoglio-becomes-pope-
francis-to-lead-catholics/

http://www.newadvent.org/cathen/14081a.ht
m

http://www.newadvent.org/cathen/06221a.ht
m

http://www.npr.org/2013/03/14/174295530/i
n-argentina-the-new-pope-has-many-
supporters-and-a-few-critics

Made in the USA
Lexington, KY
10 April 2013